A Whirlwind in Leytonstone

Michael Clements

PublishAmerica
Baltimore

ISBN: 1-4137-3941-4
PUBLISHED BY PUBLISHAMERICA, LLLP
www.publishamerica.com
Baltimore

Printed in the United States of America

This book is
dedicated to
Dr Indra S. Bhatnagar

- an excellent physician

Acknowledgment

*I wish to acknowledge the inspiration given me
by the programme "Arabian Night"
transmitted by BBC Radio Three
in summer 2004
which included many examples of
Arabic poetry, ancient and modern.*

Contents

Nights of Summer in a Deserted Vineyard

The owl, mad mentor of the lime,
plays orchard upon the hour
of celestial stealth;
shadow-night upon the ferns
chuckles juice-jay
with sweet decline;
the petals of the nightshade flower
for sleep by the river earns
more than spurt-dirt day:
the mines of slumbers ease
with distant murals
painted with fondness
and the wine-spring
purple press of sour-hour squeeze.

Bastet

I am Bastet whose heavy-lidded green-eyed stare
may make you all uneasy even when I am not there.
Now I am sick of my brothers and sisters in Heaven,
the Fat Cow with the sun between her painted horns,
the Silly Mare ridden by raggedy heroes at attention,
the Crying Croc and Unrelished Crab, not to mention
the Noxious Scorpion, and the Stinking Fish on their starry slab.
For I, alone it seems, have no star to guide me,
am pushed out on the margins unceremoniously,
with gibbering baboons, dung-beetles (I ask you!)
and seedy cobras, moulting vultures and one Wild Pig.
I once petitioned Imhotep to grant me, please,
a little margin of the sky, not even all that big,
but I never got on the official Zodiac, as the Lion
refused to claim me as kin, and even the dim Lynx
spat at me when I suggested a timeshare lease.
So I, Bastet, hung up my cat-suit in the celestial closet
one fine day and came down to stay with you, the Naked Apes
who first built our temples, and became Cat Woman,
beautiful, wicked and mysterious, and a star in my own right,
still worshipped and adored when my snotty relatives
are either completely forgotten or just ignored.

Khnum

I created life from earth and water,
and on my potter's wheel of stars
I gave shape to the worlds
on which my creatures would dwell:
and for myself I chose a home
beside the first great cataract of the Nile
where I was neighbour to lovely Isis
in her redecorated temple of Philae.
Coming out of the desert from the West,
you will appreciate the gardens
of the Lord of the Waters and raise
your voice to join my hymn of praise
under the crescent moon and the evening star,
both sacred to the pale wife of Osiris.

Master of arts and crafts, I devised the rules
of alchemy, not that bird-brain Thoth,
invented electrolysis to turn base metal
into impeccable gold, and blew glass
like a howler monkey: but the other gods
sneered at my acid-stained apron
and charred eyebrows, and bribed
the scribes with false promises of life after death
to move me down a rank or two
below that parvenu Ammon and his bad breath.

Sleeping Among Scorpions

The great temple is not empty:
snakes are emerging
from hidden rooms
in the vast and battered walls
to hunt for mice, crossing
areas of cold moonlight,
from shadow to shadow.
This place of owls and rodents,
scorpions and serpents
was rescued from the desert
like a capsized schooner
with many masts, raised up from
the rising dunes
to help us understand
the greater cunning
of our ancestors.

Daughter of the Jinn

When I was young
I married a *jinnaya* but she granted
me no wishes, preferring to sit
by the door, pursing her lips and humming.
She addressed me only to order
tea and cream cakes, or venison
and pumpkin pie, washed down with *Thunderbird*.
I had to take her to see the *Phantom of the Opera*
seven times and she would never wear
the acrylic shell-suits I bought her in Romford Market.

Finally, I had to phone her father in Aleppo,
and ask him to take her back,
as the goods were not as advertised.
This the stern giant did but refused to refund
the bride-price of seventy-seven silver dollars,
or even give me a share of the wedding presents,
which included a flying carpet I had my eye on.

I was young and handsome with a long red beard
which the ladies loved to tug,
and could have had a merry mermaid
or a giggling wood nymph, or even
a passionate Valkyrie, but no! I had to be greedy
and wanted not just one, but three wishes granted.

A Street Plan of Luxor

Does this long alley leading from the Nile
connect with the plains of Cydonia ?
Surely I have been here before, flicking
through old copies of *Astounding*, a boy
soaking up visions of the Old City,
filled with ghosts and phantoms from a long lost
past, and the canals, running like green lines
through a desert of powder and red cliffs ?

Set

With fingers of sand I carve the mound
and produce a skeleton from the rock
and watch it hop about with a clacking sound
remembering flowers and kisses
before it became a thing and not a king,
for I love the sweet disorder of Chaos,
and tricks and complex jokes make my day.
Lotus-pools attract water-snakes
as beautiful women are the prey
of old and ugly millionaires.

And, I, who simply like to shock,
summon the odd whirlwind from the crag,
madden the hippo and give cunning to the croc:
unlike the other gods, I can
peddle on both sides of the street,
quite capricious in radiant drag,
and ride the World Serpent, old
Python, to family weddings.

A Planetary Alignment

In death I should have been so exalted,
but the drunken priests messed up the mantras,
wild fists flew across my recumbent corpse,
jackal masks were knocked awry, Nebemankh,
the Opener of the Mouth, spat a tooth
out and mumbled foul obscenities.
Then the Underworld demons tore away
the blue amulets from my bandages,
tomb-robbers prized away the gold inlays
and angry peasants threw rocks at my name.

There is no free lunch in the Afterlife
any more as my offering-tables
are lost or broken, leaving me only
sublime stinks from McDonalds of Luxor
to imbibe. I've no slaves to boss about
either, as the *ushabtiw* were stolen
by the thieving French, nor hot and shrieking
chambermaids to chase about after lunch,
no glory in war as my set of black
conscripts, carved and painted by a master
craftsman, disappeared in Berlin, under
a rain of thousand-pound bombs. (Your wars
are exercises in genocide, but
mine were harmless fairground fun with winners
and losers clearly designated.)

You may ask me why I still cling on like this?
Look up there and see the stern faces
of the old gods, the gathered planets which
still rule the destiny we marked out at
Denderah on the great Zodiac Wheel,

also stolen by the French, and maybe
when some eager, charming babe consults
her glossy magazine and reads aloud
the prognostications of the Lion, Crab,
Scorpion and Ram of God, it still counts
as a prayer and keeps me going. Perhaps
for a people like us, it is no sad
fate to be guaranteed immortality
from the lips of millions of pretty girls.

Dreaming of Crocodilopolis

Not from sour Eve came our true Martian
genealogy, but from dark Lilith,
the Mother of Mysteries, her life force
starborne on a stubborn meteorite
flashing above the barren seas of Earth.
And ever since then we have stumbled on
from place to time and space, making our own
maps of the world immanent solely
in the crevices of imagination:
once on rock, like the painted travel paths
of the Saharan pastoralists when
the desert was green and full of ostriches,
and now on bits of paper, portraying
a world crowded with lines, names and numbers.

That saurian part of our brain, known at
Kom Ombo as Sobek, watches us make
sandcastles of our lives, God of Medicine,
(good work for a carrion flesh-eater),
the devourer of unclean hearts, he whose
name burns like a cauterizing iron,
and while the walls fall down, all the Pharaohs
and their armies of clerks turn into dust,
and the tears of Isis take new turns across the sand.

The crocodile in us will not let go,
and the unknowing Nile becomes
the primary river of the Unconscious,
dark, dark waters giving life to deserts
of the spirit, spawning monsters anew,
ever blessed by black women with strong sons,
ever bearing us on into star-lighted
adventures in unfamiliar caverns.

The Texture of Midnight

Spidery writing in a big book,
lots of pentagrams,
stories which ring out of rocks
and make lizards leap,
tell of the vixen from my garden
who crept into my bedroom
and sat on my chest at midnight.
The pillars of the temple have fallen:
only ghosts remain; she is
my Anubis with a tale to tell
woven from my nightmares.

Magic in Other People's Gardens

Love in broad daylight
is not a revolutionary act
when nothing is forbidden,
and smashing
the rich man's greenhouse,
is a crime against cucumbers,
but not against nature.
Rough sleepers with blazing
supermarket trolleys
will not change society,
only light up a few aisles:
the Minotaur in the sewers
will bellow distantly, but not cease
his predatory patrol.
Picking up the gnomes
is an effort for a drunk:
hurling them through glass
an added difficulty, but the ecstasy
of shattering panes, conjuring blue demons from the mist,
far outweighs the fine.

Moloch

When Adam first chased Eve and the angel
beat the bushes with a flaming sword to scare
them out, and the Serpent sniggered at their
bare singed behinds, another devil
began to build his grim towers of mud
and crystal: Great Moloch,
enemy of light and counter of coins.
As Babylon rose above the dusty
plain, with shimmering tiles and cool gardens,
palms, acacia, and little fish-filled pools,
the brazen ovens of Moloch fed on
tender flesh. Hailed for his prudence,
and the accuracy of his budgets, he
counted coppers without stop; loving bronze
he ran on oil, known to the Achaeans
as Talos, the brazen giant, he ploughed
the sad earth in his stinking chariot.

Many names and many guises had he,
the Lord of Filth, and many peoples knew and
worshipped him, an *afrit* with divine ambitions,
Moloch, the bedmate of the rich, copper
king, and king of coppers, tongue ever in
cheek when he kisses the investor's arse.
As every beast in blue has a number
so has the Lord of Brass Buttons, but his
changes every day whenever *Nasdaq*
and *Hang Seng*, his slaves, tinker with the wheels
of the world to make a little money.

If Lucifer runs on pride, and Mammon runs
on pure greed, brother Moloch runs on oil:
when the oil fails, like Talos, overcome
by the cunning Medea, he crashes
into a pile of junk. Then do the sweet
flowers of the meadow poke their little
roots between his joins; and the rich mosses
colonise his brazen innards: green rust
puts an end to his financial conquests.
Without oil, tanks will halt, Arab children
will live and his grey cities become the cold
tombs of bankers; without the amber blood
from the ocean no tyrant can survive.
Now let us build the New Babylon, with Gates of Gog
and Magog, a northern sequel to old
tales of one whose feet were not clay but cold.

Bewitching You

Thus do I bewitch you, my love, lady
of the deep mere where sedge and bulrush sleep
in autumn mists, and fleet silhouettes creep
against the moon, of November geese. She
wanders restless from her linen sheets, free
of dreaming, among ferns and the dark heap
of leaves at tree root, up on to the steep
slopes of the Hill of Stones. Devotedly
carved are the lines of faith in the green rock,
for worshippers and worshipped long forgotten:
have you rebecome the original
beloved spirit of the valley ? This clock
of old stones has stopped after zero ten
and your breath has frozen, become final.

Cat Tanka

Big spotted cat on the rooftop,
Yellow eyes slitted with bloodlust,
Half dreaming of doomed fat pigeons,
will not respond to my leftovers.

The Kind Lady

The kind lady sows seeds at dusk
on the eyes of children.
You look for her among the green chambers
of a breathing wood but that constant vision
escapes the knowledge of your eyes.
Mature autumn turns leaves to red laughter
in the rainstorm of her hair
but no new love presses her cold body
against the naked window
and the streets are empty and all the houses
homeless of understanding.
Upon the shuttle of the seasons
rests her maternal hand
moist and dark like earth.

The Dancer on the Burning Ground

In the centre of the nowhere
in which we sleep,
around which the stars swim
like motes of embers
from the funeral pyre
of the galaxy,
the father of Lord Ganesha dances
endlessly,
brighter than a Chola bronze,
blue-throated *yogi*
joyously tossing the entrails
of old stars at his brother
who recreates universes
from the glowing ashes.
And their wives,
those twin lotus jewels,
gleaming with diamond drops,
clap their hands
in time with the endless hymn.

The Writing is on the Wall

Better to drink export cider in the park
than to fight the dragons inside ASDA,
and to await the coming of the twilight
on a supermarket trolley of shining silver.
(A dragon falls from grace by good works
and mercy to the weak, and the ones
with name-tags are known in the annals of Hell.)
Barry is Jesus! has been scrawled over
the Turkish supermarket wall,
where He turned the water into alco-pop.
The tramps in the Coronation Gardens
have passed into a morbid sleep,
without hope of resurrection by a passing creep
and there is no kiss for Lazarus.

Silenus, dozing companion of Dionysus,
lies in a puddle of piss, flies gaping,
and all he can manage for prophecy is:

What goes around, comes around.
Every other bum is a fallen angel,
and I see them hopping if not flying
to rob the shelves at the End of Daze.

Having pronounced this, he puked
into the goldfish grotto and nearly drowned.

The Snow Man

Cold, he peers through my window,
with black, currant-bun eyes,
and no vaporous breath
issues from his icy lips
because he is not alive,
only animated by sinister forces
like one of Galvani's frogs.

As night falls, he seems to glow
from reflected light but remains
uncheerful. Such as he were first
created by squat Mousterian hunters
to mark their territory, and often
they sculpted the reddened snow
around a slaughtered enemy,
and placed on his shiny pate
a fresh scalp. Night is given up
to stalking monsters and among them
strides the grinning man of ice.

Fate is a Romany

Luminous-eyed lord of the pot
and keg, be a third bedfellow, and prise
apart the legs of this casual mate so as not
to spoil my advantage: do not despise
her spell of loveliness which possesses all
the heat of an August noon,
when the cicadas scrape a rusty tune
beyond the vineyards: and shadows are small
in the farmyard.
Fate is a Romany-
a black-eyed teller of tales from the hills,
visiting briefly to read palms, her skills
reinforced by *marsala*.
The empty
cup she sipped from shall I keep underneath
my grubby pillow like a touched schoolboy,
and when the vast moon rides the saddled hills
I shall cast a spell with it, ivy-wreath
about my brow, hazel-wand in hand, eager
and burning brighter, with every witless sigh
from the naked strangers along my path.
Let languorous waves linger like fingers
of flame in the sun's last flicker and I'll
make a fire on the beach, and try
to summon her.

While driftwood smoke lingers
like foreign coils among the dunes, shingles
crackle under bare feet and apostasy
turns pilgrims into (no great mystery)
dionysiacs, the menacing god mingles
blood and wine on the sand.
To prophecy
unheard during a storm is great hardship,
to drink a calabash of stars without
a toast, more than a mere lack of manners.

Rags are the New Black

One morning you will get up early
and going out the door see how
bad everything has become:
there will be bodies in the streets,
of course, but not just foreign
slave-labourers, like the Chinese
pirate-DVD pushers in their mass grave
behind *ASDA,* no, now it could be
anybody who did not go to a good school.
The wild dogs released by our leaders
will roam the streets feasting on human
brains, having tugs-of-war with an arm
or severed foot. Distantly, there will be
the rattle of automatic gunfire,
always coming closer, and overhead,
the police helicopters will fire on any crowd
over eight in number. If you are
young and strong you can join the Resistance,
and go off to be trained as an urban guerilla
in Tajikistan or Colombia,
but if you're old and weak you'll be dead,
unless you can pay off the tweeny street-gangs
with some of your state-supplied
potato-mash powder. And if you
still own an old black and white TV
you can watch the Prime Minister at play,
or looking grim on his Trident submarine,
but there's no sound, I'm glad to say.

The King, as usual, will deliver an obscene
Christmas message from the Windsor
estacion in Argentina and all will be right
in their world. Since they shot the last MP,
the House of Lords has been running those areas
designated category A, and those designated C
have been franchised to Kim Chong Il. (There
is no category B left any more, I'm afraid.)
So start planning your exit now. Don't be slow.
Buy lots of lottery tickets and scratch cards,
or else rush to prison without passing GO.
In jail they will retrain you as a paid
community torturer, or porn-channel superstar
if you have at least three convictions as a sex-offender
with boys, girls or both, even animals,
—it doesn't matter as long as you don't shirk
the challenges of out-sourcing Hollywood,
and the globalization of sex-slavery.
There will always be a place for the ambitious
criminal in the advancing world of no work.

Mr President

When I get on the bus,
the driver with a smile
leads me to the best seat,
and all the other passengers
get up in respect,
file out, and run alongside
the vehicle cheering me,
and calling upon God
to give me long life.
If they flag a bit,
my bodyguard helps them along
with a few prods from an M-16.
By nature you see,
I am a devoted democrat
and want to get close
to my people, so I
hardly ever use the State limousine,
except for public executions,
where the condemned
would not appreciate informality.

The Testament of Aquarius

Once I was fire-clad in a suit of lights,
worshipped by the builders of *ziggurats*
as their saviour in a dust dry land,
a bearded *djinn,* close kin to Azazel
and Baphomet. Then I was a perfect
boy, tipping scalding tea onto Jove's lap
when he stuck his hand up my vest, always
a handful, this genie with a water
bottle who strides the sky.
Now two thousand
years are mine, and the sad-eyed Fish can sulk.
What's in my bottle *? Piss and vinegar.*

I am the new *I* in your sky, children,
Rex Mundi, the Lord of the Air. One hand
in Kabul, the other takes liberties
in New York, one leg under the Mansion
House table, the other offshore, always
ready to run with the markets.
I am the Lord of the Air, a humming-
bird, with crocodile teeth, reproducing
anthrax and the poisonous images
of fried children in flattened hospitals:

the Fish still swim after two thousand years,
but in my personal aquarium
of blood from the stars. The Fish gave you Death,
I give you Death on TV, plagues with neat
plagiarism from great communicators,
war easily explained, sometimes stern and
awful to be kind, famine engineered
to bring babies to their senses, and all
scientific, rational and truly
aquarian. What's in my old bottle ?
Empty echoes in a vast, desert space.

Taking Tea with the Dragon

Summer soothes the sounds
of bees with books
and the grass covets
the feet of a foreign princess:
time folds the hands of the clock
over XII.
Crickets mimic cantos
in the willow-garden
and the prince from Cilicia
and the dragon break from combat
beyond the Tartar Wall
—a horn sweetly summoning them
to the tea-taking,
shared with beggars in the shade.

Master of the Lightning

You may wake me from sleep,
calling on the cold north wind,
but I do not fear for teeth in the dark
and my shabby pillow of ferns
holds my spirit steady in dream.
Some days I can feast on cheesecake,
and others keep holy by fasting,
and some days can trudge many miles
and others dedicate to meditation.
Many are envious of this pilgrimage,
hating their mired lives,
and curse me when I dance to the slow
music of the Pleiades, but being
a seventh son of Mother Earth,
I am Master of the Lightning
and can read whole histories
in the charred stumps of trees,
and find nuggets of gold
turned up by the thunderbolt.

Arcades and High Towers

Always paying with fairy gold
and leaving the greedy with a headache
in the morning, on Hampstead Heath
I talked to Blake who listened to the breath
of the stars and was silent. If you
find me a beggar at your door,
or lonely in the prison with a prophet's dreams,
or peddling death in some forgotten desert war,
invite me in to lead the prayers with a toothy grin.

Just look up when the full moon weaves
jigsaw patterns through the lattice, and star
upon star points the heavens, and a far
dog pack howls for bitches, and call my name.

On a night for thieves and exhibitionist lovers
I seek to steal the breath from the wicked
and the blood from the veins of the smug.
I exist only to limit your ignorance of the dark
and to nibble at your slavish obedience
to the light which consumes all, at least for a time.

The Bag Lady Up West

The marble idol high above the Strand
speaks to the bag lady in the doorway
of the grilled-up tobacconist's: she may
nod occasionally, raising her hand
to sift the Word of God upon the land
bright with neon lamps, but she'll never say
her own word. The Son of Man she'll obey
forgetful of her own sons, and the bland,
blank eyes will consume her sight, night after
night, above the pigeon-shit tears. Shuffling
about Stoke Newington by day, laughter
on soiled wings above her grey hair, ruffling
the air, beyond all despair, she sees all
Eden Grove poised and poisoned for the Fall.

A Variety of Loving

We make love separately
each on his own side of the curtain
with a mirror-reflected image,
a simulacrum of crystal flesh,
so that I never touch your hair
when the porcelain possesses
the gentle feel of genitals,
and the essences of the belly
dry in the sterile air.

The Meditation of Merlin

This form which grins before my tower door
mayhap may claim my soul for evermore
if I forget the last secret of love
in love's embrace: to give old Death a shove
out of bed and shake off his nipping claw.
In every diamond lurks a fatal flaw,
so they say, and my lover's velvet glove
may willfully squeeze below and above
and tweak me between pain and sharp delight,
yet fail to provide continuity
in the sweaty urgencies of the night.
When all's said, there's a superfluity
of bones and ashes, insufficiency
of sighs and creak of the bed's symphony.

Vision

Athena rests her hand
on my left shoulder.
She is my guardian spirit,
though I have always known her
as the *Achni Devi,*
the unsleeping watcher
at the Gate to our world,
or Kali, grandmother of the Roma,
named as Samsara,
the first daughter of Maya,
Lord of Illusion,
who could not divert Gautama
from the supreme path.
Older than the life-flowering lotus
of Brahma, born
not from fire but from spirit;
and I see her secret knowledge
shine in the eyes
of all beautiful women
when I look at them.

Temple of Apollo, Pompeii

The wall is rough here now, Encolpius,
where once you kissed the pretty Gito—
and the scenes of the sacred mystery
have flaked and fallen from the dim fresco:
the archer god still draws his string-less bow
at the black branches of an olive tree
with a moonbeam shaft—for divinity,
even its form, aging in stone, ages slow.
The crumbling of a wall is nothing
to love which outlives copies of copies of scrolls
of hopeless verses, deep in our reborn souls.

Building the New Babylon

And where else should we build
the New Babylon but on the barren
purity of Cydonia's plains?
Under great glass-fibre and teflon domes
the nine metre tall camellias will
blossom at the feet of Liberty and
butterflies the size of bats will circle
her dreadlocked head. Not from sour Eve will come
our Martian genealogy, but from
dark Lilith, the Mother of Mysteries,
and our women heroes will be bad girls
all: a brave host of Calamity Janes
with the proud, fierce heart of Lola Montez
and the intellect of Cleopatra.
Splendour will touch the rose craters of Mars
with a fresh dawn from which are banished
crosses and dull fathers ratting on sons
to the cops, coin-counting bourgeois battening
on the poor, our greedy, worthless
ruling class made fatter yet from public funds:
avenues of sphinxes with smiles and breasts
of stone metamorphosed by volcanic
fury will lead to our sacred plazas
where freedom's statue rules: for we all are
the people, more numerous than the stars
in the indigo sky of Mars, wiser
than any ambitious president, and nobler
of heart than any smug monarch.
Let our thunder reach to Heaven, and let
our ships have new names like the *Carmen Jones*.

Infrequently Three-headed

This particular goddess is all arms
which she uses to squirm her way through
the thick forest: she may approach from behind
without warning and tip you over
with practised ease. One hand will stifle
your screams for mercy, while another two
will pull off your trousers and underpants,
and another take a firm grip of your private parts.
From one mouth will come unbridled giggles,
from a second a long red tongue will emerge
to lick the nape of your neck,
and a third will whisper of outrageous
love-positions and tell salacious tales
of her ambushes of respectable males.

Elsewhere

We walk arm in arm through patterns of cloud
while rain closes shutters on the restive
forest, and the trees make
a noise like groaning above the secretive lake.
Mist fills the haunted, fathomless
shaft of the long dead volcanic abyss,
and reeds silently guard their knowledge
of ancient sacrifice: behind us ridge on ridge
the lava mountains march with foreign names
like dragons, their true births written in flames.

Homo Crudelis

The Tattooed Man was the first true human
to make a sacrifice to gain magical might.
He put on the skin of a slaughtered foe
and danced grinning in the moonlight,
full of hate with horns on his head,
and called a severed heart a blessed flower.
He fathered a new race of warlocks
who made calendars of stone, and books of human hide,
who look like us but prefer the secrecy of the night,
liking to live in cellars, though a cell often serves;
a tribe fascinated by knives, though they cannot
work a bellows or make the black iron flow,
and leap to loud, unfamiliar sounds, though they cannot
play a drum or make a flute bring the reeds to rustling.
They wear the tattered finery of our lords and ladies,
though they never toil and are inept thieves,
live in the ruins they create from our dwellings,
and ever hold themselves to be aristocrats in sad
exile from some lost country where murder rules,
rape is the only honest relationship, and to be mad
is the path to freedom from the custody of fools.

Acid Rain May Fall

Do not wear a leather coat today,
because the wind is from the north
and acid rain may fall.

Do not use the underground today
because the signals are busted on three lines
from the incessant acid rain on the old wiring.

When I see your cute face staring from the bus
I know you are not searching for me
and my tears are not salty, but acid.

Do not eat your sandwiches in the park,
for the pigeons have taken cover
and acid rain may fall.

Jaggery Goor

The time has come round again
to march upon the Jaggery Mart
with our blood-red banners
of festival and its dizzying joys.
Beat the drums of *shagreen* leather
and toss the plumed lances high,
put your shoulders to the high-wheeled cart
of world conquering Jagannath,
throw aside your introvert manners,
dance until your elbows tremble
and sing until your noses bleed.
I've seen before Dionysus lead
his coterie of naked girls and boys
along the littered High Street
and past the market stalls,
through dismal rain on frozen feet,
but today will resemble
a Vrindavan noon.

And Dionysus said to me
between tender kisses and smiles:
"Eat the *goor* and drink the *bhang*
and let the *thyrsus* bounce
all in honour of our festivity.

From the endless aisles
of the bountiful Jaggery Mart—
this sunset is a new circus born
for those who seek immortality!"

And when night comes the dead will rise
on bat wings against the crimson skies
and none will mourn,
and none will mourn.

Medea

This cloak, embroidered with the black venom
of my hate, will consume like fire and oil
together.
My tears mingled with the toil
of that dark loom into the cloth, and from
that wooden nest of frame and needles some
spell self-wraught entered weave of mating coil
on coil, phoenix on salamander.
Boil an old fool for the sake of a kingdom,
being productive of ghosts! Sew them here
with hair from a golden head shimmering
still with his hot kisses, and persevere
in revenge: the slut who dons it, giggling
and ambitious, will feel dragon's breath
on her flesh.
With bright, burning loins comes Death.

Kookoo Sabzi

The doors of the Turkish supermarket
stand wide open and I must hunt
for *jaggery goor*
so that I may pour
its sublime sweetness
over my lover's tongue.
I shall not leave this life
until I've wrung
every joy from the *Chef's Pillow Book*
underlined in red.
Open your coral pink lips,
my sweet,
and taste this treat
on a nest of ginger,
with almonds scented,
and fried in *kookoo sabzi:*
better even than
the tapioca pudding I cook,
or the ducal bubble and squeak
which we'll munch contented
as ever at the end of the week.

Missing the Bus

Because of her tears
she could not see it and failed
to put out her hand.

Pan

I zoom between the universes and dimensions
on a clapped-out Harley-Davidson
in a leather-jacket with Yogi Bear on the back,
and I really do have horns on my head,
but not cloven hooves inside my riding boots,
as that's Faunus, a Roman lookalike.
No, I am an Arcadian, apart from being
every nationality at all times, and I am
amused to have *Olympian* as occupation
on my Hellenic diplomatic passport.
Zeus adopted me, you see, so I have to work
twice as hard as those born in the purple.
I faked my own death for a lark,
and stood in for Hades as ruler of Hell (temporarily)
when he went visiting his cousin, Yama.
I kicked out that squatter Lucifer and his gang,
but some idiots still insist I am the Devil—
it's the horns, you see.

I was the god of the slaves for a long time
and that tends to change you,
(ask Baron Samedi if you want another opinion.)
I protected them from their Spartan masters
as best I could. If runaways could make it to the hills
I would lead their blond pursuers astray,
lost among the thickets and dwarf oaks,
and put them and their huge dogs into a *panic*.

My great scream once shook all time and space
and drove the Titans into Tartarus, pretty quick,
though some insist it was just an asteroid
annihilating the dinosaurs. Quite a trick.
It all comes down to the same thing, though:
I saved the gods from them and allowed
the creation of a new world for the clever apes.

I have no temples and my shrines
are funny-shaped rocks beside quiet pools,
or gnarled oaks blackened by lightning.
Lao Tse dubbed me *Uncle Waterfall*
because I rose from hidden mountains
and refreshed the earth with wisdom's fountains.
I am loved still in the East
where they call me Hanuman,
or Monkey (because of my hairy, australopithecine face),
and it was I who protected Tripithaka
when he brought back the sacred scriptures.
I am the oldest and wisest of all the gods,
and when I play the rogue at Hell's portal.
I am merely contacting my inner human.

And in all those aeons before the now
I only once lowered my head in a bow
before another, and he was mortal,
and lived in India, and was wiser than any god.

Banners of Red Silk

Banners of red silk emblazoned
with black characters greeted our passage
through the narrow streets of Xi-An.
A good-time girl smiled at me
and coming out of the throng
told me to beware a feeling
of self-satisfaction in completing
our arduous and painful journey.
We had struggled every inch
of the way against demons
across the high peaks,
but now, on the flat lands,
began a new contest
against ourselves, which none
would witness or applaud.

I looked at her closely
and saw it was Monkey in drag.
"We all like a joke," I said:
"but I feel your heart
was never in our holy mission
to bring back the *sutras* to China."

"Monk," he replied, "Just remember
that I spoke with the Enlightened One
face to face, a thousand years
before your birth."

"Huh! And what good did it do you?
You still gaze after a plump backside,
stuff yourself with prawn balls,
wet your whistle with rice wine,
dance and fall about after a few,
and return a blow, not with wise words
but with the tricks of an accomplished
boxing champion. The Master would weep!"

"The Master would laugh like a drain!
For I knew him and loved him,
and he was no dry scholar
or sly, priestly hypocrite.
He was the son of a king,
a warrior fearless in battle
before he renounced the path
of relentless conflict.
All our feet are on the way,
and the great work of our poor heroism
lies not in bringing the *sutras* to China,
but in following their teaching.
Om mani padme hum."

And with these words the girl left me.

Ska

Disco is the music the gods dance to,
in my room, every Friday nighty.
Though Baron Samedi is a boogie man,
and I prefer to ska with Aphrodite.

Child Slaves of the Aral Sea

Waking from an ugly dream, the girl lay half-comatose
staring up at the grimy ceiling paper,
twisting a strand of night-black hair around her nose.
She was bored with her new caper
in stuffy Chelsea where the *nouveaux riches* pout and pose.
The local youths were middle class football wankers,
junior accountants, management trainees
or else the languid sons of merchant bankers.

She glowered at the poster which hung by her bed,
pin-holed by darts, left behind in the flat.
A frowning Regina smiled upon five Corgis, about to be fed.
Four looked expectant, but one with lolling tongue gazed up
with an expression which plainly said:
"I've just pissed in your coffee cup,
dear monarch. What do you think of that ?"

With a ripping noise the dog sprang from the poster,
and landed on her stomach, quite a breathtaking blow,
leaving a torn space, crumpled and black, in the royal suite,
and a familiar voice filled her head
and the bed
rocked like a roller coaster:
" *We must act at once! The Tattooed Man is back!*"
"Cerberus! Is that you ? Are you on a job *incognito* ?"
But her face was being licked in a doggy ecstasy
and she had to wait a mo:

"When you blew him up outside The Baker's Arms
his discarnate soul eluded the Furies by chance
and entered the body of Yagma Katilov
the Russian billionaire and greedy bastard
driving to Stansted to catch a flight to France. "

"But all that was ages ago!"

"Only six months which he has used to lie low
to escape detection by the Furies Investigation Bureau.
Now we have to stop him from getting new boots, ring
and magic belt from Katilov's factory by the lost Aral Sea."

From her cupboard she pulled out the tatty sneakers,
and the twist of rope, once a magic girdle, but
the ring she had pawned (not cast into Mt Doom)
and sighed: "These have lost their *va-va-voom*."

"Put them on," said Cerberus, *"for the power*
is in the wearer, not the stitching or the fancy loom."

And so it was. For once on her feet,
the sad old things became Seven League Boots,
as in the tales of old, and within the hour
they stood beneath the Leytonstone Midland Railway Bridge,
dreary miles to the east from the city's fashionable west,
where Cerberus sought an old friend to join their quest.
For in that alley close to the Turkish Food Centre
dossed one of the world's legendary heroes, mighty Herakles,
and his adoring wife, ex-cocktail waitress to the gods, sweet Hebe,
both flat out recovering from a Dionysian bender.

At her feet, the girl found a ragged, snoring bruiser,
feet bare, his red-gold curls hopping with happy lice,
a fresh black eye bearing witness to his bare-knuckle agenda
outside the pub last night with a mortal loser.

"O heavens, he stinks like an open sewer, and his bitch, too"
gasped the girl with a tissue over her nose.

The rats turned away from the chicken nuggets and crisps bags
and looked at her as one demented. The giant opened
bright blue eyes, and croaked, " Medea! You've returned, my rose!"

"Not Medea, *Mave*. And please don't breathe on me!" she spurned.
Cerberus had in his teeth an ancient rolled-up carpet
discarded in the alley which he dragged over to the bleary hero.

"This is a genuine Bokhara carpet which can be made to return
home with us upon it—help me, old friend, and off we go!"

But when Herakles had it open, Mave (as we now know her)
gave a high-pitched scream: " *Look at it!* It's covered in enormous fleas!
And how can we sit on all that rat piss ? We'll get Weil's Disease!"

Cerberus agreed and took the lead. A few steps away stood
a car-wash and from this emerged some moments later
a naked girl bearing a soaking carpet behind a naked lout,
and a dog with detergent bubbles in his snout,
shaking himself in a fit of spray. But the manager full of wrath,
ran after them into the street:"This ain't a public bath!
I'll call the cops if you don't pay, you hippy layabout!"
He jumped up and down in a childish huff.

But Mave's face remained haughty and tough:
"Now, if I sit on that wet disgrace, I'm sure to get piles."

Patient Cerberus scratched his nose and thought, *"Then*
while I dry us all off through the portal in the supermarket wall,
you go into that charity shop across the street and buy
our friends some clean stuff as they attract attention in the buff."

Mave liked to shop and crossed the street
where traffic had come to a sudden stop
at one glimpse of public nudity. Tall Hebe was easy to kit
with a long grey skirt, red calfskin boots and dark blue top.
But huge Herakles was not a regular size.
So she bought him, though sad to fork out her hardcomeby coin,

an African *dashiki* for a shirt and a baggy pair of leather
alpine hiking breeches reinforced in the groin,
made in Rosenheim for a famous tourist, very unfit.
To clad his feet all she could find were a pair of rope sandals.
For herself she bought a black beret with an egret's feather
and a silver brooch of Gothic design to pin on it.

A crowd gathered to watch the nudes, now dry
and with clean hair free of tiny guests, get dressed,
but the carpet smouldered in places, and smoked in others
because Cerberus had used the portal on the sly
to sneak back home and dry it in the very pit of Hell.
The clothes suited the wearers and even fitted well,
though Herakles was puzzled by the inscription on the buckle
of the belt for his breeches: GOTT MIT UNS,
but Cerberus laughed and said it was true for once.

Then from the cop-shop a few hundred yards away
down the High Road, at last issued the reply to the manager's smear:
fifty *muckras* bearing shields in full riot gear,
and waving their batons high, chanting in chorus:
"Down with the nudes and their indecency,
(we can watch them later on the CCTV).

And any who do not disperse, will catch it worse;
Brazilians will find it an open season,
and be cruelly shot in the head on suspicion of treason."

"Look at those Babylonians, little blue men with little blue dreams,"
grunted the great hero "I must set to nought their wicked schemes."

But the malevolant car-wash manager cat-called with a sneer,
"You'll catch it now, you raving Greek queer!"
And the son of Zeus, picking up an empty rum bottle
replied:"Then catch you this on your way down to Hell!"

The bottle flew like a lightning bolt and pierced his skull,
filling up with the brains which he'd not used well.
Flat on his back he crashed, like a demolished siege tower,
His eyes rolled back to show the white, a truly hideous sight.
"Ya-Iaou-Yi!" roared Herakles longing for his sword of shining bronze,
and its leather scabbard stitched with ivory plates
bearing images of bloody battle and lives cut short by the Fates,
his high helmet with the scarlet horse-tail crest,
the Sarmatian fish-scale armour gleaming on his chest,
his chariot and his bow-bearing archer friend and lover,
adding beauty and courage to the tales of sanguine discord,
and picked up a rusty tyre iron to make remarkable his final hour.
"I loathe clubs," he muttered: "A warrior lives by the sword."
His blue eyes blazed and his golden curls stood out from his brow,
and Hebe added her war-cry:"*Defend your cubs, O women of Hellas!*"
to his, so that the pavement cracked and the sky went black
and the shades around the war memorial stirred in their long vigil,
remembering how once on the Somme they had massed for the dawn
attack.

The frenzied crowd turned and ran on to the police shields full of fear,
fighting to escape, but were beaten back, giving time to the four
to board the carpet. *"Let's go, Mave!"* commanded Cerberus,
and when she looked back blankly, impatiently added:
"I can't order it to fly as I am weak and like a dream here,
while really asleep in my kennel beside the adamantine door,
and our divine passengers are incarnated as human poor,
so only you, who once lived as the mighty witch, Medea,
can direct this disinfected rug to the Aral shore."

Feeling foolish, but quick-witted as ever, Mave made up a verse:
"Rise up, good carpet, and bear us in safety to the mystic East,
where we are bound to slaughter a wicked beast,
free the infants made despairing slaves,
and save them all from early graves"

There was no sense of movement, but all outside the carpet's rim
became as though made of mist and very dim.
Moments passed until Mave sniffed the air and without turning,
remarked,"Can any one else smell burning ?"
Hebe screamed: "My bottom! O, my bum is on fire!"
Herakles laughed, thinking it a sly invitation, and replied:
"Then I'll take my ration of your passion!"
Mave heard movement behind her as the hero swept Hebe on to his lap,
but turning saw flames around them and ugly coils of smoke .
"You idiot!" she hissed at Cerberus: "Why did you have to stick
it in the flames of *Hell* ?" And the carpet fell apart around them as she
spoke.

Herakles moved up as more of the rug burned away
until Hebe was crushed against Mave's back, but neither lover
was prepared to stop their rhythmic jig-a-jiggling,
and Mave cursed herself for not buying them knickers,
though even iron-plated ones would not have been too thick.
"Hebe," she grated,"stop nibbling my ears"

but it only set Hera's wayward daughter to giggling.
There was a sound like a car crashing its gears
and the mists around them vanished, revealing the desert
a mile below, and before them the blue of the shrunken sea.
Mave swept the dog into her jacket and zipped him safe,
as the carpet fell away from their sizzling rears.
"We're going down," she grimly said: "hang on to me as we fall.
I still have the boots," and Herakles put his arms around them all.

The inertia made them sail on a bit, then start to descend.
Hebe and Herakles loved the thrill of the ultimate rush:
and set to join *The Mile High to Ground Zero Club*, even if dead,
and Mave also expected to die until she saw on her left
a great eagle, golden and glorious, bearing in its claws
a disconsolate green serpent, which the eagle flung at her head.
Raising a hand to ward it off, Mave felt it tighten around her wrist,
and saw it was now a bracelet of precious green jadeite
which seemed to glare at her from blood red rubies for eyes.
Then the eagle was beneath her, greatly grown in size and might.
Her left boot slammed against the wing with a metallic ring
and they were all propelled forward again as by a spring,
right over the cobalt waters of the salt-poisoned sea.

Again they began to sink, and she expected to drown in the drink,
but now from her right appeared a man-sized monkey
with a shining crown as he steered a surfboard of cumulus cloud,
and grinned at Herakles with his breeches around his ankles,
and to Hebe, with her skirt up above her waist, gallantly bowed.
As they started to plunge another two thousand feet
he pulled from his silk waist band a little black rod
which grew and grew until Mave's magic boot on the right
struck it as a mighty pillar, and they shot forward again.

They lost a little speed before they began again to dive
many miles short of the original shore-line,
over an area of quicksand and shale and patches of salt,
all bad and *very* bad, so that she heard the monsters in the mud
make sucking noises in anticipation of their blood.
But there was a ship! An old rusting ferry canted on one side,
abandoned as the sea shrank back, with one firm spar on the wreck
reaching up sixty feet from the bridge. But however Mave tried
to manoeuvre her boots for a jump, she still saw a gap
of at least a yard. But then she glimpsed movement on deck—
a beautiful dark-skinned boy with a wreath of vine-leaves about his brow
who played a lingering refrain on a flute which made her sad
and also joyous, meditative and sleepy, drunken and mad!
At his bare feet stretched a huge black panther, and at his side in despair
wept a fat old man with a fringe of dirty white hair
about his bald pate. As the boy played the ska classic *Special Brew*,
huge vine leaves swarmed up the tilted mast to close the yard gap,
Mave's foot connected and they bounded forward from the trap.

Now only twenty feet above the slime and broken rocks,
the scattered girders and collapsed concrete of useless docks,
Mave saw ahead a line of dunes and shouted over her shoulder
"When I say BREAK!, roll each to one side avoiding that boulder."
She unzipped her jacket and Cerberus jumped free.
Amazingly, he seemed made of paper and floated down safely,
and when she gave the word, Herakles relaxed his grip with a sigh
and rolled to the left, and scarlet-cheeked Hebe to the right,
just as a sudden gust of wind from the cheeks of Boreas
filled the lowered breeches and the spread skirt,
so that the golden pair were deposited breathless on the dirt.

Mave was twenty feet above the ground diving out of the blue,
head-first like a human cannonball straight at a rock.
She'd never survive the impact, she knew, as she flew,
but then two thick tendrils of vine sped out of the wrecked ship

and wrapped round her ankles like ropes of elastic
so that she came a fraction of an inch from the boulder
and then was wrenched back with a groan, like a cracked whip.
So shattering was the shock when she at last struck the sand
that she blacked out and lay still, face down, clutching vines in her hand.

She came close to strangling on the grains in her nose and mouth
but Herakles clapped her on the back until the stars
came down from heaven and whizzed around her head.
Bruised and shivering she returned from the dead.
Comforting her with an extended lick, the little dog said,
"Our destination lies beyond this dune.
We must get a move on before day turns to night."
"I'll reconnoitre," announced Herakles," for none will see
my approach. I know well this place having dwelt here
with a hot Scythian snake-dancer for three idle years in exile.
And as an Argonaut, I was often assigned to scout and poke about."

"He'd poke Scouts, too, given a chance" added Cerberus with a waggish smile.

But Mave was gaping up at the line of soldiers who'd appeared
like ghosts on the top of the dune, though she need not have feared.
They had come to surrender, not attack, being as much slaves
as the children making shoddy clothes fourteen hours a day.
Most were older brothers or sisters, a few parents, all
refugees from the wars and rebellions which forced them to stay.
As they walked to the barracks, the sun cast their shadows
like pointers home, and out of the north roared a man possessed,
and two helicopters, unmarked. The larger disgorged men
in camouflage and black ski-masks, and to Mave's dismay,
they bore *kalashnikovs* with a familiar ease. From the smaller craft
emerged, wearing a Savile Row suit, a middle-aged clerk,
his eyes dull and lifeless, like those of a shark.
Mave and the others stood frozen in the main courtyard,
and above them children's faces pressed against the panes.

When Katilov saw Mave he choked and ordered his guard
to mow them all down, but a strange scent filled the air
and bright blossoms floated in on the breeze. The soldiers threw down
their arms and began to drift off looking for flowers to pick.
So the billionaire rushed at Mave with a flailing right fist.
Herakles and Hebe were stunned by his speed,
Cerberus sprang like a hero but was felled by a kick
only Mave deep in her memory knew what to do.
Slipping the bracelet from her blue-veined wrist
she cried,"Nobody kicks my dog!"and hurled it true,
and it encircled his throat, shrinking till he turned blue.
So greedy Katilov died kicking his heels like a felon hanged,
and his wraith still haunts that expanse, but the body rose up
with the Tattooed Man inside still bent on revenge.
"This is it" she thought, unable even to take a step
of seven leagues, so fixed by his glare, when who should glide
from the shadows but the naked boy from the wreck
with the panther and the mad old tramp, and stand by her side.

In an attitude of adoration, legs apart, arms outstretched
stood the gaping old man like an "X," or that hero from Goya,
defying his end, a funny old bloke weeping fit to choke.
Katilov's corpse stopped its attack and said only,"Master!"
It fell to its knees, repeating the word in a dreadful croak.
Herakles and Hebe began to pick falling blossoms out of the air
and make each other chaplets, loving and sweet;
but Cerberus showed his teeth, snarling at the panther
whose tail was lashing a treat.
"Medea, it's you I want," said the youth:
"You're just the one to complete my court, and revel
uncontrolled with the rest of my girls when we join a film festival
and scream like transvestites in a naval port,
or lovers in a phone-booth, interrupted by a giant white bunny,
so join me, bow down and give it me, love me like a rabid uncouth,
and I will free the children with a kiss, a hug and a signed photo,

and throw the Tattoed Man into Hell, where he is meant to go.
I'll also give you back the memory of making easy money
from souls who like a good show, a bit of blow,
and doing the naughty in public when the action gets slow,
as you once did in Hecate's temple, my moon-struck honey."

"Never!,"cried Mave:"I know what you are, master of tricks,
while some enslave for money and power, you do it for kicks,
and feed off the sorrow of your weak and helpless addicts!"

The youthful god, enraged by rejection, swore to cash in her chips,
but Mave was quicker than any bent card-dealer as she tore
the belt,
yes,
the magic belt,
from about her hips
and hurled it at Dionysus, the dodgiest dealer in the blue,
Demon Drink himself, come to earth to make a score,
recruit new disciples and raise the dead for a start.
It snaked around him faster than any jungle liana, up to his eyes,
and bound him in its implacable bonds like magical superglue.
High overhead the circling eagle gave a shriek of surprise,
the panther made to leap but Cerberus, no paper tiger,
growled as the Guardian of Hell, and Silenus pissed himself with a fart.
The Tattooed Man stumbled forward to save
his ensorcelled lord and play a conclusive part,
but it was twilight when gods may be slain or wrongs righted,
and Mave held out her hand and Python, that old serpent,
left the dead man's throat and flew into her hand.
She cast it at the feet of the shambling, livid corpse and cried,
in the ancient tongue of Colchis, "Let the teeth
of the dragon feast on this offering, and strip his bones bare!"
Python, the hungry World Serpent, rose up and took
with relish his struggling and screaming prize,
swallowing the damned soul in a single gulp like *fondue*.

(The Furies arriving late again, unsure what to wear
like teenage schoolgirls, going at last for the Valkyrie biker look,
heaved sighs of relief, and flew off to an all-night disco in Baku.)

"Those girls," sighed Cerberus, *"have lost all interest
in law enforcement careers, and will go the way of the Fates."*
For that lazy trio had long ago fled to a fun life with Club Med.

Then Python looked at the struggling Father of Drunks,
gave Mave a significant glance, while she thought it through.
Dionysus was able to free his little finger and squeak,
"You wait a moment, and I'll turn you all into fast food pulp!"
And Mave said, "Eat the fucker!" and old Python obliged.
As the god slithered down into the serpent's belly,
the circling eagle uttered a last sad shriek
and sped off into the folds of relentless night,
while the compound generator kicked in amid hissing sparks
to bathe the courtyard in mind-numbingly brilliant electric light.
Silenus leaped up and ran off to the desert, wailing,
"God is dead! God is dead! And the booze has all run out!"
(He ran all the way back to the Leytonstone Midland Railway Bridge
where the cops tried to frame him for the *Rum Bottle Slaughter,*
and the subsequent *Nude Terrorists Riot.*
The charges failed, but a year later he was almost nailed
for the *Great Hypermarket Trash and Carry,*
which he had planned with Lilith, the Devil's daughter.)

The black panther gave a cat-like shrug
and sauntered over to Mave for a friendly hug,
while Cerberus said, as the cheering children sped
down the stairs to greet their redeemers,
*"Come, old friend, our work is done here despite the schemers,
and we can go home and rest."* And Python
shrank into a green dog collar with an audibly happy sigh.

"Just a minute," growled Mave as the spellbound dreamers
started to look about with a sleepy but puzzled eye,
"First he helps me, and then he turns nasty. May I ask why?"

*"Zeus came out of retirement to help catch the Tattooed Man
but also to prove his superiority over my true master, Pan,
but when he divined your identity as Medea,
he told Dionysus who only pretended to enable our quest.
All along he wanted to trap you as one of his cult,
like Herakles and Hebe, because of your undying fame
as the most powerful witch in the west.
There's always a new fake along, like him, claiming to be
the truth and the light, and the sole way for all Eternity,
puffed up with ridiculous pride and filled with poisonous enmity
for all those who reject his empty claim.
When you defied the wretch, and had him cast into Hell,
Zeus could do naught as we are placed east of the Urals
beyond which his Olympian writ does not run. But just as well,
my master, the Great God Pan, oversaw our fight
in his form as Monkey, who has jurisdiction here by right."*

At that moment, a cloud alighted at their feet, from which
stepped Monkey, to the delight of the children now
swarming about them. But while they saw only his simian grin,
Mave saw an Arcadian peasant, small in stature, and with wrinkled skin,
and, of course, the horns. Pan ordered the factory guards
to pick up the snoring Russians and store
them somewhere safe, without their toys, and make them behave,
adding, "Keep the pilots separate." To Mave he said more:
"If you look in the smaller aircraft, and you need no clues,
you will see a large metal box which is your Aladdin's Cave, dear Mave."
The trunk she found was plain in sight but the key to the lock
was now inside Python and Mave had to use
a blowtorch from the factory workshop to cut it open.

It contained one hundred million US dollars in greenback bills,
passports issued by countries in Europe without fear or favour,
without photos and names, plus contracts signed by government ministers,
with letters of thanks from satisfied friends in New Labour.

The two helicopters took off in the morning with about
a quarter of the children and adults aboard,
each compensated from the discovered hoard.
This left one hundred and twenty souls stranded.
There was a train which brought in supplies,
but it wasn't due for a month. While the freed slaves
(and Herakles and Hebe) looked for new wardrobes
in the packing shed, Pan, Cerberus and Mave made a pact.
They couldn't wait for the train in this prison, but had to act.
For the money would buy a brand-new life abroad.
The twenty Russians would be given cash to keep
them quiet and could fly home when their pilots returned,
but the freed slaves were too many for that.
So Pan opened a portal for every mortal in a rocky ridge,
out of sight where the sheltering dunes lay steep,
and they went into Tartarus at one place,
and emerged safely in another, in fact, by the Midland Bridge,
while Cerberus bounded off to his kennel and Python curled
about the roots of the world, knowing the god would have to be purged,
but giving it an aeon before Dionysus reemerged.

Some idlers noticed a file of blindfolded children
and adults bearing bulging gunny-sacks
stumble out from the supermarket wall,
(for no living mortal may gaze back on the Underworld
and live—remember sad Eurydice and her terrible wrong!)
but thought it a school outing like a mystery tour,
though the smell of sulphur was a little bit strong,
and the huge black cat with them snarled at the throng,

and others were more flabbergasted, if not struck dumb,
by the heliotrope shell-suits of Herakles and his matching winsome.
Mave, of course, found with pitiless flair
a rundown stately home in Essex at auction, where
she set up the *Aral Sea Orphanage and Private School*,
all the way greasing the palm of each Rotarian fool.
And the huge black cat made Epping Forest her lair.

Freed from the sinister cult, Herakles never reentered a pub,
and became the new, reforming Headmaster,
as firm in handshake as Arnold of Rugby, with Hebe as Deputy,
a step up from her last job to tell the truth.
And she kept his mind off Scouts, being Goddess of Youth,
by having them found a not very respectable sky-diving club.

Local Elections Jazz

We promise you fresh vomit
in every alley, and thieves and beggars
determined to amuse
in every bus station.
Every pensioner with a handcart
may apply for household rats
at Walthamstow Town Hall,
though you must take all abuse
from the surly staff
in good part—it's just a laugh!

A *Dog Shit Bride of the Year Contest*
will be held again in every ward,
so bring your buckets.
(It's cheaper than confetti,
and helps the environment.)
Small children will be taught
how to roll in dog shit,
and older ones can show their bent
by competing to join
the *Dog Shit Skittles Team*,
soon to be an Olympic sport!
Waltham Forest is thus well on the way
to realising another dream—
to become the 2012 European
City of Dog Shit.

The formation clog-dancing team
has won an Arts Council grant
to take their street ballet
O to Wallow in Fresh Dog Shit
to North Korea,
on condition that they never return.
This is, however, unlikely
as the penalty for anti-social *traits*
(like gobbing on the pavement,
pissing in dark shop doorways,
vomiting outside restaurants,
and, my own favourite,
encouraging your doggy
to leave the footpath ankle deep in shit)
is *death*.

Afterlife

Next time let me be born
somewhere where the men
have thick black moustaches
and wear red fezes with tassels,
black suits, and heavy boots,
drink thick coffee from small glasses
and stare glumly into bigger glasses
of ice-cold water, chain-smoking and
wondering whether the railway track
to the capital will be cleared of rocks
before the end of the week.

For I'd like to wear a cummerbund
on velvet evenings and flirt
with watching Parisian starlets
as huge tankers swim past the pasha's palace,
and run through the streets with others
waving a sabre on rare occasions
of civil emergency. Most of all,
I'd like to lock up my reckless women
at the back of the house where they can sip
green tea or sherbet, and feast on honey cakes,
cinnamon sponges, and tiny, sticky tartlets.

Tartarus

When the Great God Pan let out his scream
and drove the Titans from our time and space
they were given Tartarus as a residence
and for them it was like a Spanish villa
for a retired East End gangster, or contract killer,
being the same world as this but bigger,
more undeveloped, hotter and steamier
around the equator but colder and harsher
in the polar latitudes. A place full of monsters
to hunt with wobbly, flint-tipped spears
and barbecue over molten rock, for the Titans are big,
with hard muscles and mighty thews, hale and hairy,
and need their protein fresh and bloody.
They love lots of exercise, wrestling, boxing,
shin-kicking and head-banging, followed by back-slapping,
brawling, biting, gouging and testicular horseplay,
all in fun, and in their quiet and reflective moments,
they often fill an idle hour with bar-billiards,
skittles and mead, quaffing while their womenfolk
dance to wild music or pick lice from each other's hair.
Unfortunately, they are addicted to playing stupid, dangerous
games with edged weapons like *The Unfaithful Wife Test*
which involves throwing axes at your tied-up
spouse. This rarely leads to real bloodshed
because all the other women surround the man
waving their own axes and spears in his face,
telling him that this treatment is a barbaric disgrace.

The Titans love their new world and now would never leave,
but resent its use as a dump for recidivists
like Tantalus and Sisyphus, or a holding cell
for Olympians, and remember how Herakles,
friend and saviour of noble Prometheus spoiled his
spotless reputation by throwing Hera,
his own quarrelsome future mother-in-law down among them
without a by-your-leave, or even a proper court order
issued by Hades, their original link-man with the sky-born,
(though he was never around, and you had to talk to
Minos or Rhadamanthus to get anything done.
When Pan was appointed Viceroy, he closed the border,
kicked out that squatter Lucifer, and recognised
the Titanic Declaration of Independence,
but that came later, when it made a lot of sense.)
The furious Hera created so much trouble and complained
so endlessly about the violent weather, the heavier gravity,
the sulphur in the air from the exploding volcanoes,
and the giant household pets like Echidna and Hydra,
the affectionate Kraken in the public swimming pool,
and the especially the thieving Cercopes, also dumped by Herakles,
that the Titans appointed a deputation of Helios,
Hyperion and Tethys, who finally had to drag her
back up to the Adamantine Gates and throw her out
bodily: "And don't come back!" added Tethys, which is
a terrible thing to have to say to a guest, even if uninvited.
Scowling, she aimed a kick at poor Cerberus,
missed and cracked the wall of his kennel,
frightening his half-grown pups and enraging Mrs. Cerberus,
and then picking up the folds of her Tyrian purple dress,
rushed up the narrow stairs immortalised
by unhappy Eurydice, and burst into sunlight out of the Pit,
shrieking, "Curse you Herakles! Now, you'll
never wed my daughter, Hebe! Ha!"
But she was hit

by a privatised sanitation truck, which to humanity's distress,
could not harm *her*, but exploded, drenching
her and the passersby at Harrow Green with sewage and stenching
slime. Sitting and stinking in the bus shelter, she gaped
at the amazing changes about her, the *automobiles*
and the pyramid atop the Canary Wharf tower,
for one short month in twisted Tartarus
counts for five thousand years in our time.
Beside her sat a sad old fellow with a cane, dressed in jeans
and a shabby leather jacket, who advised her to clean up
in a nearby car-wash. "It's just a *station* that way," he gestured
with his stick," but try not to kill anybody, even if they kick
up a fuss, or happy-slap your bare bottom." Raising his hat,
he bowed his bald head, and was rewarded with a nod.
On the way she realised that he had spoken
to her in that archaic form of Greek which we see on rare
crocks and jugs and call linear B, but did not really care.
True to form, the new manager at the car-wash was a cad.
He sneered and then made threats, and looked for a camera,
as Hera stepped out of her sodden dress like a Greek goddess,
but his wiser men screamed: "It's another one!" and ran like mad.

Iakkhos, Iakkhos!

I have crushed a cheap pearl in vinegar
and added the cooled essence of bay leaves.
I shall swallow it down when the moon weaves
jigsaw patterns through the lattice, and star
upon star points the heavens, and a far
dog pack howls for bitches.
A night for thieves
is this, and I'd steal (from one who believes
in gods foreign to me) circumpolar
kisses.
Luminous-eyed lord of the pot
and keg, be a third bedfellow, and prise
apart the legs of our mate so as not
to spoil our advantage, do not despise
our romping but get stuck in.
This you owe
to us mortals who make your vineyards grow.

Vanessa

Twelve trees are one grove not to be passed by,
providing shade on a hot day: and there
she will find the badge left by her lover—
carved deep in hazelwood, on May's Eve, nigh
to midnight, with a new flint from the thigh
of fat earth. Some sweet spirit of the air
will whisper cantos in her ear, and her
lips will find a new tune to fancify
the spell of youth. —Come, cool pallid limbs
in the bounty of this bright pool, mistress
born of Pleiades, red-haired enchantress,
and toss your silver bow above the rim
of the dreaming valley. You have woken
the last, dark name from sleep, and it is spoken.

On Wanstead Flats

Weskit Jack lived by the Pond,
no longer young, but full of ambition
he experimented without contrition
on drunken maidens, stolen by night's gloom,
within the confines of his laboratory room,
and buried the bits in a nearby dune.
Now, thanks to a full, swollen harvest moon,
and heavy rains out of season, the Pond
burst out its banks, laying the evidence
bare in the morning's light.

Like a dark and dreadful presence
of evil he seemed in his bowler hat,
as he walked to TESCO's to buy this and that,
quite oblivious of the looks of hate
directed his way from every gate,
until Lilith, the Devil's daughter,
intent on robbery more than slaughter,
cut his plucked chicken throat
with a broken bottle, stole his hat
and all his money, and bought a used *Alfa*
with his platinum card. Moving into the flat
of this wicked old goat,
she changed all the locks, sold his organs
on the Internet and bought a leopard skin coat.

Many a wild party she flung, with her beau,
fat, old Silenus the Bulgarian sot,
and the randy satyrs at that spot,

until celebrities began to flow,
to what they dubbed a "lakeside retreat."
The press called her a veritable vamp
as she never wore knickers and had a sneer
so aristocratic that any politico, MP or peer,
would find his groin suddenly damp.

"Darling," she purred on Channel Four,
"Born in Babylon, I'm older than I look,
and Daddy was advisor to Saddam Hussein
but is now out of work and on his way down the drain.
I've been promised a place on *Celebrities from Hell*,
but it sounds rather vulgar, and a bit of a bore.
I'm wicked, as you know, quite rotten to the core,
and I'm not a good sport, quite the reverse,
for I just have to win, whatever the sin,
and I won't be beaten (unless it's perverse)
so there can't be a contest if I put all rivals to rest.
Still, rather than mope, I'll choose a good grope,
but if men displease, it's really hard cheese,
'cos then I have to tear them off a strip."
Her wide green eyes had a penetrating stare,
numberless admirers were numbed by her spell,
leather-bound ministers were strung up for a taste of her whip,
cardinals and bishops imploring, all wanted their share,
and tired businessmen readily agreed to a clip,
but no more young girls went missing at night
which really rather made it all right.

Sacred Landscape

"Satan will be free, my friends" can still be seen
scrawled on the walls of the Turkish supermarket,
and we may also note Lilith, the Devil's daughter
and her beau, the alcoholic Silenus, with his satyr chums,
forcing the Chairperson of Sexual Services to her knees,
during the Spring Festival on Harrow Green,
her protesting voice drowned by the flutes and drums.

Towards distant Canary Wharf the light breeze
wafts the smell of burning sandalwood
and I assume that the coupling bums
are excited by the accompanying stench of blood.

Imagination is the new philosopher's stone
transmuting the silence of the urban wasteland into
shrieking sacrifice and stained exploding bone.
For this is the borough where, turning a corner,
you get jumped and publicly degraded by a leather-clad
trio of Furies, a motorcycle gang on speed;
where you may be surprised after dark in the public lavatory
by gremlins, who demolish the building around you,
then run off with your trousers, so that the police not only
pin the damage on you, but also arrest you for indecency;
where rats the size of dray-horses run down the High Street
with screaming babies in their jaws,
and give the finger with their claws;
where they put up marble statues to car-jackers,
and put fulminate of mercury in the Christmas crackers.

Until my death (alas!)I shall have to wear a cloak of feathers
and a mask of alluvial gold sieved from the river
by Midas himself, so that Lilith will think me
one born from the cinders of a dark star, like herself,
and not rob me in broad daylight, or cut out my liver.

Crimson Sunset

My vixen comes and goes
through night's sombre shadows,
but I have left her no scraps:
some dustbins will collapse.

Foreign Words in the Text

Greek names are represented in the Latin spelling convention:

Silenus, *not Silenos*
Dionysus, *not Dionysos (and definitely not Bacchus)*
Hephaestus, *not Hephaistos (and definitely not Vulcan)*
Cerberus, *not Kerberos, etc*

However, there are two exceptions: Eros, whose name is spelled the same in Latin and Greek, is once referred to as *Cupid,* and Herakles is always used instead of *Heracles* as a heroic exception, and as *Hercules* never.

In the same way, Odysseus is always used, and not *Ulysses.* Though in modern Greek this heroic name is pronounced *Othisefs* which is sort of between the two and suggests that the Greek taught in Anglo-Saxon schools is grotesquely mispronounced, and rightly causes the Greeks to fall about helpless with laughter.

The Romani word *muckras,* meaning *bluebottles* or *cops,* is used in the long poem *Child Slaves* and is a degraded dialect form of *makkhre,* which means *flies* in all the North Indian dialects to which Romani is related. Maybe Mave should have thought in Shelta, the Irish traveller language, but my father's language is a mystery to me as he was killed in Normandy two years after my birth.

I later on use *rozzer* which may describe a policeman as a *rozlo,* an old word for *tough guy.*

Sanskritik names related to the Hindu gods and places sacred to them, and words related to Buddhism, are rendered in a form of phonetic spelling widely adopted in general books on mythology to avoid the dots and dashes and acute accents used in more scholarly texts. Old imperial spellings from the days of the British Raj are avoided: thus, Vrndavan, not Brindaban.

Egyptian gods are usually referred to by their Greek names, such as Isis and not Wa'aset or Thoth, and not Djehuty, apart from Set who was known to the Greeks as Typhon.

Chinese names are transcribed into the official *pin-yin* Romanised script, not Wade-Giles—thus Lao Zi, not *Lao Tse*, the founder of Daoism, not *Taoism*.

Printed in the United States
60329LVS00006B/112